FRANCES HOROVITZ
COLLECTED POEMS

Frances Horovitz

COLLECTED
POEMS

in association with the
ENITHARMON PRESS

First published 1985 by
Bloodaxe Books Ltd,
P.O. Box 1SN,
Newcastle upon Tyne NE99 1SN,
& the
Enitharmon Press,
22 Huntingdon Road,
East Finchley,
London N2 9DU.

ISBN: 0 906427 86 X Bloodaxe Books hardback
0 906427 87 8 Bloodaxe Books paperback
0 905289 54 4 Enitharmon Press hardback
0 905289 49 8 Enitharmon Press paperback

Bloodaxe Books Ltd acknowledges
the financial assistance of Northern Arts.

Typeset by True North, Newcastle upon Tyne.

Printed in Great Britain by
Unwin Brothers Ltd, Old Woking, Surrey.

Acknowledgements

This book includes poems from the following collections by Frances Horovitz: *Poems* (St Albert's Press, 1967), *The High Tower* (New Departures, 1970), *Water Over Stone* (Enitharmon Press, 1980), and *Snow Light, Water Light* (Bloodaxe Books, 1983).

Acknowledgements are due to the editors of the following magazines and anthologies in which a number of the uncollected poems first appeared: *Anglo-Welsh Review, New Departures* 7-11 (*Big Huge*) and 16 (*A Celebration of and for Frances Horovitz*, 2nd edition), *New Poetry 7* (Hutchinson/Arts Council – P.E.N., 1981), *New Writing* (West Midlands Arts), *PN Review, Poetry Review, Whales: A Celebration* (Little Brown, 1983) and *Writing Women*.

'Avebury', 'Chanctonbury Ring', 'West Kennet Long Barrow', 'Uffington White Horse' and 'Glastonbury Tor' were commissioned as part of a series of cards on ancient sites by Gallery 5. 'Night-piece' first appeared in *For David Gascoyne on his Sixty-Fifth Birthday* (Enitharmon Press/Ampersand Press, 1981). 'Solstice Song' was the last poem to be printed at the Piccolo Press. 'For Adam, nearly twelve' first appeared as a poster from the Five Seasons Press.

The frontispiece and cover photograph is by Mike Golding.

Contents

SNOW LIGHT, WATER LIGHT (1983)

VOICES RETURNING

UNFINISHED POEMS AND FRAGMENTS

Editor's note

Shortly before she died, Frances asked me to see her final collection through the press. It was to be called *Voices Returning*, and was to include her last poems, all the poems in *Snow Light, Water Light*, the six *Rowlstone Haiku* we had written together, and a number of earlier poems not collected in *Water Over Stone*. In the two years since Frances' death, interest in her work has grown to such an extent that it rapidly became clear, both to me and to her publishers, that we should proceed directly to a *Collected Poems*.

In order to show the development of Frances' work, I have grouped the poems chronologically, under the titles of her successive collections. The poems in each group do not, of course, correspond exactly to those in the original volumes. The details are made clear in the bibliographical note but, briefly, 'The High Tower' includes all but one of the poems from the original volume, plus two poems reprinted from Frances' first pamphlet, *Poems*, and one uncollected poem; 'Water Over Stone' includes all but one of the original poems, plus eighteen uncollected poems from Frances' ten years in Gloucestershire; 'Snow Light, Water Light' reprints that volume complete, except for two poems written in Gloucestershire, before Frances moved to the North, which now take their rightful place in 'Water Over Stone'. No reprinting of *Rowlstone Haiku* could match their presentation in the beautiful Five Seasons Press edition, which is still in print, and so I have omitted them. Frances' last poems appear, in accordance with her wish, under the title of 'Voices Returning', together with the dedication she had chosen for that projected volume. There follows one further group of 'Unfinished Poems and Fragments'.

These groupings provide only a rough chronological outline. Within each group the poems appear in thematic sequence rather than in order of composition. In one case I have allowed thematic sense to prevail over chronology completely. 'Old Song', which appears in 'Water Over Stone', was in fact one of Frances' last poems, written in May 1983. The experience it recalls, the same experience that is recalled in

11

'Written in the Black Mountains', makes it an integral part of the sequence of love poems written from 1975 to 1977. It has, on one level, a narrative function in that sequence, and I have placed it accordingly. But I mention that it was written in Frances' dying months because that adds quite another level of meaning. The 'grief' that 'birdsong and water bear away' is more than the grief of lost love. That earlier loss becomes a rehearsal for the present loss.

Frances wrote sparely and sparingly. She was such a severe judge of her own work that I have thought long and hard before omitting anything she herself had allowed to enter print. Only with a handful of poems did I face any real difficulty of decision. Some omissions have been made in the light of Frances' own misgivings: others because the poems, though well-made in themselves, seemed of a weaker imaginative pulse when read against others in the collection. The work set its own standard and such few omissions as I have made have served only to clarify its achievement.

Occasionally the text in the *Collected Poems* differs slightly from the text of an earlier printing. These changes are based on Frances' own subsequent corrections, either made in manuscript or in discussion with me. The text of the *Collected Poems* is the final and definitive text.

The editorial judgements are mine, and the responsibility for them must rest with me: but I would like to express my thanks to Gillian Clarke, Paul Hyland, Tessa Lund, and Anne Stevenson, all of whom gave me the benefit of their critical insight at various stages of the selection. I would also like to thank Michael Horovitz for his help in providing me with copies of manuscripts in his possession, and with information on the date of composition of some of the poems.

ROGER GARFITT

THE HIGH TOWER (1970)

*for Graham and Zoë
and for Michael*

Allegory

they strip me and cast me out

at the city gate my love a hawk hooded
his eyes dark under the arch
or in a high tower behind steep walls
his arms raised in a corner of stone

a frail wind hurries the brown leaves
small lights grow dim
the sun darkens
spears spring up around me
my white back a beacon to his eyes
distant in tall grasses

his hands fall like the young moon
touching my flesh in shadow only
in the black wood I am no longer seen
thorn bush, dried reeds, stones in the river bed—
they bar your steps with spears that cover the sky

Winter Woods

air hangs like metal
two swans shrunken
on yellow water
red berries—omens
we cannot decipher
a green leaf startles
                    like blood
whose bones beneath the tree?

we walk—cracking the silence
the daylight moon stares through branches
leprosy invading iron

our warm blood stills
the sun is livid in exile
we have encroached—
this is not yet our land

Women

women
lie open
as green meadows
to the urgent flood

compassion
for the erect member
and hand trembling

over shoulders
gazing
at different wallpapers
compassionate
and lonely
as the travelling moon

Do you not know that I need to touch you
as I touch a fruit or child?

Knowledge I need of you that comes not
                                with words.

Let me touch your hair, your moving lip,
the bone beneath the gentle skin.

I will not harm you—I do not want your sex.

Trust me to touch you and to leave you whole.

Morning Waking

casually perfect
        as a leaf or shell
upon white sheets you lie
emblem and cipher of yourself

your lineaments are royal
        as those of ancient monarchs
                upon coins

and as remote
        as those dead kings
                from my seeking eye.

this morning

    he walks naked

       in front of me

last night

    slept easily

       by my side

these more precious

    than declaration

       or mating—

your silence
   spreads like water
      in an empty room

limp flowers
   in cellophane
      your gift
their scent rises
   a thin column
      leaning towards me

black trees
   barricade the sky
each morning
   we are ambushed
      by birds

your skull echoes

an inexhaustible fountain
   of sound

Loving You

soft as old silk
I tread in this room
wary of space
that between us flows
you know me
as fish knows fish in tide—
no more you know
I could mark you through to the bone—
no touch
you'd own
so gently I walk
around the space
enclosing you
soft as silk
loving you

London Summer

high flying
tattered flags
of blue and white
a Tiepolo sky
over London streets

and we—
summer kites
borne gently down
to the warm pavements
at peace—
stretched frail and luminous
by the passionate freedom of the air

Love Poem

your total absence
rehearsal of my death

in this game
there is no substitute
all symbol gone
the knife flicks home
for real—

moon is
    eye of the fish
discarded littoral
    that nightly swims
into our room
    cast up
in cold proximity
    we lie
on our deserted shore
    tide is
a bone's echo
    leaving us parched
in the noon sun
    we reflect
the vulture's eye
    clearly
to each other
    we mirror
the inexorable circling
    our virtue
endurance only

this Eurydice made it—
fragmented, bloody
an unattended birth
forced out between rocks
in a barren field

the light sears

where are the flowers
the song's echo
in the season of spring?

only the voices of others
lamenting also
the shadow of Orpheus
stretching always
    over the hill
      over the hill

Bird

leave the bright voices on the edge of the wood
follow the bird quick
     arrow—messenger—
into the still shadow of the waiting trees

     light falls from leaf to leaf
     spattering gold is leaf is light
     and bird
     shadow swift
     falls—follows
          the air—speeds
       in shafts of green
       vanishing invisible
       as echoing song ahead

     trails silence in the choir of trees

brown moss quiet underfoot
sunlight glitters in the empty glade

Crow

hieroglyph between hills
inheritor of high trees
sudden wreckage of silence
cry alien among birds

ragged wing flap
startling the calm air
deceitful dalliance
black spy in the land

guardian on post and wall
watchful each in his own field
in beady surveillance
cottage and dark wood

Buzzard

our connection is silence
   the plunge in the blood

what music he moves to—
   he plays me
from the bed of the lane
he reels out my sight
he turns round the hills
eddies   splits air
lounges like paper
he drops the whole sky

a comet too near the earth
   rabid he crashes
   yellow eye glittering
   savage his absence
   scoring the fields

leaves hang in stillness
a breath drawn   suspended
our connection is silence
   the plunge in the blood

Spell

already
you people my night wood
       with birds
     their infinite pipings
         veining the dark
I called to you
       out of the tree
    from your own brain
       I answered
I would change shape—
     in a cauldron of ichor
   entering your bones
      look out from your eyes
and see only myself

Moon

city bred
   I watch the moon
      through glass

distorted beyond vagary
   she rides
      the accuser
swinging tides
like recalcitrant skirts

her solitude breeds memory
heaves it to birth
mocks the still-born

moon, I remember—
your light a scalpel thrust
from a mouth of white bone

even through glass
I mirror your loneliness
walking in warm rooms

—sometimes I wish you
no more than a thumbprint
on the edge of the sky

Dunskeig
Hill of the Fort

hill stillness
bee's din left far behind
shadow surging in the grey grass
eye follows empty sheep track
—final struggle up the Pictish stones

      there
      stand in sun's harness
      see as they saw
      the small dark men
      body of white water
      lain open to the sky
      bland—calm—
      to the hawk's eye
      but to the watchers
      bitter intricate tides
      bearing blood
      and sudden fury

islands glimmer
      constant in the shifting haze
nearer—rocks
      strewn at the world's beginning
home of the harsh gull

tide's caul stirs the brown wrack
colder seas call this inland water
      resting between hills
seaways for longboat and saint

but in the clear noon light
now as then
      our eyes may rest
the primal world is still
only the sun burns
and the expanding moment

we know those ancient watchers
    beneath the hill

Dream

dark room hurtling into dark room
leaves running under the rain
long ago my cry passed you
do not stop me now
I turn the maze of the leaf
light in a kaleidoscope shaken
cold eye of a bird, berry, wet stone
water under the earth
light existing in darkness
from the closed eyelid seeping

dolphins leap at the foot of the cliff
black between white leaping
faster
faster
slip on the wet grass
catch at the cold rock
I cannot hear you
the sound of water shouts between rock
the whole earth streams to this point of the sea
I run with the dolphin
I run with the sea
I have outrun darkness
do not stop me now—

WATER OVER STONE (1980)

for Michael and Adam

Spring

moving in sunlight
      the old adam
           in the green wood

over my body
      a web of water
           rill upon rill
               his hands sing

the old cry
      from the dark furrow
           from my blind mouth

seed to the sun springs—

Haiku

buckets filled with elder blossom
—such drunkenness between us
shredding petals for wine

two extra in our household—
a butterfly
          clings to the green curtain
he stays for winter only
the new child
          a guest for many seasons

Child in Cornwall
(for Adam Horovitz)

in his thrush-warm skull seabirds bleed white over the streets
their feathers drifting like knives
swan-boat and dragon in a whirlpool of stone

in an old house upon old stones he stands
colliding the sky with the bird
cows jump out of the oracular fields
the purple flower is the heart flower
its juice is distilled in his mouth
he sings with the sound of the fox

in his night-bed he floats up the long hill
over his eyes in water, his spilled cup spreading tides
his body the one white wave riding the ship
into the dragon harbour and out again
under the black castle on the stone cliff

in his hands the dead walk timeless in the wind-ridden grass
he has scattered their door-stones with flowers
and pried out the mouse bones from the ancient hearth

his veins are consumed with light
they flare out to the sun
as he runs over the straight roads to the space of the sea

through his mother's green ring he calls home the tide

he has answered the stones

he whimmers in sleep
for the blood-rocking of the endless boat
and a white bird crying over the white sea

Invocation

Like a whale
              let me sleep
falling through shoals of silence
imponderable, vast
displacing darkness upon darkness
pricked by oxygen of dreams.

Like a dolphin
              let me wake
plummeting toward that pellucid skin of light
to break through with laughter
ridden by your joyful thighs.

Sea-horse

Holiday trophy from Cornwall
he lies in cotton wool, fingernail long.
Obsidian eye glitters.
He is light as a husk, fragile.
Embryo perfect
he seems not dead, but waiting.

My son weeps at his strangeness;
Pegasus and mermaids are more familiar.
Except in dreams we do not remember
his watery meadows,
the undulant winds of his prairie.
Is it accident we bring him here
to limestone hills?
Creatures of his kind rise patiently
age after age toward the air,
the spade fragments them,
we kick them up at every step.
Certainly, thrown out as junk,
he will become dust with them,
his particles will ride the fields in summer air
—a resurrection, briefly, into light.

In Painswick Churchyard

'Is this where people are buried?
I will not let them bury you'

     He picnics among tombs
     —pours imaginary tea,
     a yew tree his kitchen

'You will live with me in my house'

Oh could I believe the living and dead inhabit one house
                                   under the sky
and you my child run into your future for ever

Fable

a mirror hangs in the apple tree
'photograph of no one'
     says the child
as a wind blows
and sky lies shattered
in the wet grass

Avebury

a child laughs in the bright sun
shadow of cloud on stone, on grass
birds drift from the tall elm . . .

echo of music, of dancing
footsteps wind on the serpent path
they move lightly, invisible
in the great dance among us
touching with stillness
bird and shadow and child

Chanctonbury Ring

oh lady
    crouched in a cold room
do you stir with the summer leaves
    and the singing of birds?
oh lady of darkness
    in your earth dress
      your water dress
do the blind roots
    awaken your bones?
oh lady
    what is your dream?
you who walk in the moon's path
    in a dress of chill air

West Kennet Long Barrow

enter the throat of darkness
follow the word
      winding to the heart of the stone
the dead welcome you
listen, their skulls echo with silence
          their bones sing
they have trodden the long path
         to the threshold of light
they burn with the star and the stone
they are one with the bird and the wind

Uffington White Horse

black waters swirl from your hooves
hills roll under your bones
your belly a surge of the wind
ride faster than storm, white horse
strike fire to the earth from air

Glastonbury Tor

the dance moves in us
we turn to the measure of stars
      of the hidden waters
we follow the bird's flight
      and the song
           always beyond us
the shifting of leaves is our music
our pattern the shadow of cloud
we dance to the sun
on the white hill we dance
we dance to the stillness
      at the heart of the dance

New Year Snow

For three days we waited,
a bowl of dull quartz for sky.
At night the valley dreamed of snow,
lost Christmas angels with dark-white wings
flailing the hills.
I dreamed a poem, perfect
as the first five-pointed flake,
that melted at dawn:
a Janus-time
to peer back at guttering dark days,
trajectories of the spent year.
And then snow fell.
Within an hour, a world immaculate
as January's new-hung page.
We breathe the radiant air like men new-born.
The children rush before us.
As in a dream of snow
we track through crystal fields
to the green horizon
and the sun's reflected rose.

Resolution at the New Year

Children drag home through dusk,
week-old snow brown in hedgerows,
a full moon slices the wood.

Somewhere spring is gathering its green,
star gives place to climbing star
(they too have grown older).

I shall not be careless this year:
I shall not forget to see the wild garlic blossom
—as I did last May, and the May before.

Poem of Absence

to be alone for a month is good
I follow the bright fish of memory
falling deeper into myself
to the endless present
the child's cry is my only clock

yet your singing echoes in corners
who clatters the red tea-pot
or opens the door with a bang
to look at the evening sky?
your typewriter lies silent
it is reproachful
I cannot make it stutter like you

I sit in the woods at dusk
listening for the sound of your singing
there are letters from a thousand miles
you wrote a week ago
like leaves from an autumn tree
they fall on the mat

it was your voice woke me
and the absent touch of your hand

Letter to be sent by air

the child calls from the apple tree

birds inhabit the air
their morning cries have entered my dream

through branches the child shouts at the sky
declaring its portents
his face has revealed them
the clouds are already hurrying him away

my fingers move across a vast table
encountering papers and money
bread heaves under a damp cloth
daily the house empties forth strangers and friends
our detritus is burned
we are renewed each day
a fine smoke shimmering the young leaves

sometimes my head is a lightness
filled with dry grass
I spread into the sky
over seas and wide forests
to find you
how you are torn out of me
a cry not my own splits the wind
I am streaming with air
where are your limbs in this whiteness?

in the night intervals
as speech to the tongue
I am near to you

as blood to the earth
I conjure you home

Solstice Song

imprint of metal
in a sharp sky
burning burning
this midwinter moon

unsteady
my candle flame wavers
offering of smoke
in the dawn frost

all day
birds huddle
in the leafless wood
on a black tree
the huge sun is forked

our breath
trails white flowers

sluicing of owl cry
to the cold stars

blaze blaze summer moon
the night phoenix rises
its feathers have blinded us
we stumble in whiteness
flowers turned to ash

August Full Moon

gorged moon
devourer
all night I turned under your knives
fields shine with your redness—
you have made me
a bladder, a husk
to bang lightly
what air or brightness
should I contain?

you wake me early without purpose
to boil water, cut bread
to expiate?
you have taken my words
all month I have waited
what gift is withheld?

the child has a red ball—
under his hand
it curves like the moon

Storm

grass heaves
heavy it bunches at field's corner

riding the leaves
birds cry at dusk
frenzy climbs the tall elm

out of our stone cottage
                           we sit
back to the strong bole
                              juddering
tree's labour is ours now
wood swings to the wind
                           hill turns
night is a fierce sea
                          scavenging

dawn we lie with branches fallen
earth exhausted under a still sky

Lament

petals of elderflower, dog rose
drift in the long grass
dissolution of summer—
our fixed stars decline

meeting in gardens
cool air between us
in lanes at dusk
moving apart

only the fire holds us
our flame echoed
in crumbling forests
centuries away

Night-piece

the moon has fallen on her back
night cannot console her thin belly
she ravens shadow

fires flicker and crumble
ash scudding lighter than snow

my hand a cupped moth clinging
in the folded dark our breath rises
a grey bird among pines

desire is formless between us
we are enormous as stars

last light withdraws over the sloping field
trees deep in their darker selves

your fingers stir in the black grass

memory of absence . . . .
the galloping shadow on the sky's rim

For F.E.H.
November 1904 – July 1975

the child says
he will not die
cries for magic
in his secret corner

the old man
stretched on his bed
is already summoned
weightless
as shaved bone
he will fly

two hands
cradle his head
fulcrum
between worlds

Elegy

—No, we were not close
nor had we been for years.
Too great a harshness intervened,
accusation, anger.
'A clever daughter gone downhill' you said
—at best accustomed enemies
signalling hopefully
in a bleak landscape.

And now you weep before me.
With wasted arms you draw me down
till, legs strained,
I fear to fall onto your white bed.
Your pursed old-man's lips seek mine,
you say 'Forgive me'
and I cannot think for what

—nor what comfort I may give:
to talk to you of death
hopeless, an intrusion.
I do not know your faith, nor mine
nor what god you remember
from choirboy days,
your Sunday Christ
soon cut to size
by weekday rent unpaid.
I see you now in a sepia photograph
with other ragged boys—
the sharp pinched faces
of the thriving poor.

'Stay in your own corner,' you said,
'don't let them knock you down' . . .
Did you stay upright in your narrow life?
All I know is, by default
you taught your daughters how to glean for joy.

On high pillows your head lolls sideways,
flesh fallen from the bone,
eyelids half flicker open.

I see how like you
I shall become.

Envoi

Sorting your clothes
　　　—shirts, pyjamas, socks,
my mother saw you once.
I could not ask
　　　'How did he seem—
in shining whiteness?
—Young, or as he died?'

I wear your sweater,
　　　see you faintly now:
or in the mirror
　　　as I touch my face
a stain of grief,
　　　the hidden ghost.

Poem

odour of dust
of delphiniums
lingers three thousand years
in the closed tomb
pharaoh also
mingles his scent
with the flowers

falling leaves
lodge in the child's hair
colour so like
I cannot distinguish
hair from leaf

dust of the universe
sifts into our rooms
our lives
death travels before us
—with the great stars
beyond our own dark
we are hurled

Elegy for the Mummy of a Young Girl in the British Museum

Cleopatra,
daughter of Candace
of Western Thebes,
in the second month
of her twelfth year,
stopped her breathing
—the papyrus does not say
what date or season.

Dried berry beads scattered in the hot sand,
blue and white dress by the river,
white flowers in your hair.

Buried with the Book of Breathings
at your head and foot
(spells to propitiate
those crocodile and jackal heads)
and instructions for
Traversing Eternity,
you leave behind
your faded flowers,
the wooden comb
and string of berry beads.
The painted sky goddess leans down
to take you in her arms.
What birds fly with you,
ibis or swallow,
we do not know
nor how light the feather
to weigh against your heart.

Quanterness, Orkney   3500 B.C.

Not blood, but fact, from stones and the sieved dust.

'Most die at twenty'
        —syllables snatched by wind.
Died of bone's ache, belly's ache,
        the ninth shining wave,
or long attrition of the absent sun.
'Before the Pyramids, this death-house
was the centre of their lives'.
Equal in death,
man, woman, young and old,
laid out for carrion, their wind-scoured bones
heaped hugger-mugger in the corbelled dark.
'Some rodent bones were also found.'

Each desperate spring
winds drift flower-scent from off the sea;
lambs call like children.
In warm heather
the young lie breast to breast
seeding the brief sun into their flesh.

Womb-hunger to outlast the stones.

Celebration

you are my truth teller
     come in a new year—
your bird mask clacks over the wild wood;
I could not detain you
     in gardens, in orchards,
your songs dance in my throat;
in the first month
     I sit under a tree of green fruit;
a word spoke in my mirror,
     you will return

in a picture book
     I see the dark god
     follow the maiden
     he draws near
     in shape of hewn stone
     a grey cloud in flux
     a thorn bush empty of birds
     heedless she walks
     treading on flowers
     flowers fall from her breast—
that book is closed

crowds shuffle on pavements
past buildings
that belch ashes
and the stench of bone;
holy words
like water
gone underground

the day after midsummer
a full moon stood still
on the falling spire;
the child slept
in a queen's lap of bronze;
the rune
irreversible

to be stripped of my skin
        is not enough;
water, clear, trembling,
embraces the earth
enters its secret place
is its dark vein
        flowing—
air, boundless,
consumed by the fiery tree;
your smile darkens the sun

'a knight riding
        seeks death,' you said
the poet died long ago
the old man coughs on his bed
your music summons the sea

Song

Dancing, we made music
              for our further dance;
this they cannot deny
              nor subtract ever,
those that draw black skirts
              to the dusty wall.

Lock each door behind us.
In the white cottage
              your nakedness imagined,
or a flame of ivory
              I pass through in dream.
Lie on the cool bed
              scented with lemon;
windows gaze into other rooms
the stairs will not betray us
—I awaken early
              purged of daylight longing.

On the steep path you carry me lightly.
I glimpsed you, oiled and gleaming,
              through grey leaves.
I bring flowers to the lady of foam
              and the fluted shell.
You have been here before me;
with bloodied feet we enter her darkness,
a hard measure
              danced to the bone.

Visit to the British Museum

You take me to the room of clocks
to see some long-dead master's
sleight of mind and hand.
Time thickens here, revolves,
regards itself in mirrors;
almost, each minute holds its place.
You tell me why one second hand
moves forward and not back,
explain escapement or the dead-beat pendulum.
All stars and days are measured here—
I think of loving and the seepage of our lives.

The Assyrians next;
a king hunts lions in bas-relief,
has hunted now for near three thousand years.
Would we be lovers beneath such brazen skies?
We swelter in the blood and din.
Time traps and baits us like these lions;
our moment is as transient as theirs.

So few meetings . . .

We meet in streets,
museums, others' rooms,
whirled in a blind eddy;
our true direction
dark, unknown . . . . .

I reach towards you,
disturb another's ghost.
Your dream is mine;
what we both seek
I cannot give you
for your own—
you look beyond me
to your lost land.

We may not gain
each other's self,
nor truly meet;
yet touch
most tenderly
with mind and hand.

There are so few meetings
with ourselves . . . . .

Communication—

A postcard from the mountains.
'Love to all', you write,
disdaining particulars for the general mode.
You love us all—
such kindness numbs, appals.
Where you holiday in packaged, glistening snow
I would come as fire, as revelation beast,
and fuse our bones to the unmelting rock.

Old Song

       Birdsong outside my window
recalls tremblings of water.

       I lay alone
deep in ferns by the stream's edge;
only the bee's hum
and the labyrinthine murmurings
entered my mind.

       Birdsong and water bear away grief.

I walked home through the mountain mist
       calling your name.

Written in the Black Mountains

stepping delicately over the stream,
wading the same bracken,
grass wind-blown gold or grey,
I meet last summer's self
who called out here her rags of grief,
human transitory loss . . .

I lie alone under the alder tree;
water and stone make their same music
wind shakes equally shadow and leaf
that bird hangs timeless in the streaming sky

what self have I
among these primal things,
who cannot yet distinguish
longing from love?

An Old Man Remembers

'. . . and Gwdion and Math made for Lleu Llaw Gyffes a wife
out of the flowers of the oak, the broom and the meadowsweet
and her name was Blodeuedd. And when she betrayed her
husband with Gronw Bebyr, Lord of Penllyn, for punishment
she was turned into an owl . . .'
from THE MABINOGION

in this valley she walked
                    I remember
a woman with the smell of wind in her hands
walking at nightfall in the floating dusk
veiled in the petals of an early spring

they say she was made of flowers
flowers yellow and white
                    of spring and summer
and drifted away on wind and water
when the shape spell dissolved

certain she was a flower in our valley
her breasts were flowers red and white
and her eyes and the scent of her
and certain there was never a warm child in her arms

but she lay in her lord's bed and was loved
she bore him his cup and his meat
gold was given her, white linen
and many songs by the firelight
of longing and pride

the valley contained us
a flower for a queen
lust swelled our harp strings
we grew fat on our dream

now I remember
her shadow swims clear
there was blood in the valley
                    a stranger
blood in the bowl and the spring
red sullied white
two lives destroyed
and white petals scattered
in a cold racing wind

some say of that frail woman of flowers
her love turned her to owl's wings
and lonely now in the valley
with foxes and ravens she rules

and certain at nightfall
when the owls cry out
I think I see her clear
a white shape on the hill
—but this is an old man's longing
a shadow, a dream
a memory of harp-song and flowers
and a fair woman walking in the spring

Poem in Spring

turn away from the window—
in the dawn light the language of birds
is a fine instrument
        to lodge in your brain

who photographs the dead lover?
he hangs in the apple tree
my retina holds him in his one gesture
        diminished to silence
he falls endlessly
dew drips from his hair

I follow the passage of water
petals and debris trapped in the vortices
does the same water flow always?
it glitters white over the stone
the stream is racing the sky
my arm plunged to the elbow
        will not delay it

lean into the galaxies of flowers
they are trodden and crushed
torn from my skin

Journey

now is the time for walking in woods
by the cold stream come from the waterfall
are you afraid?
                no but the path shifts
here I am safe
                but the path shifts under my feet
I walk on but the leaves are black
                and grab at my face

I remember the carriage
                craning impossibly
                      by the side of the waterfall
there was no shifting—
                the firm boards
                    held us together
                          over the waterfall
but all that is past

I saw the long steel slip into the groin of the roof
their feet clumsy but quiet on the ancient eaves
I screamed I knocked into furniture
like a bat I blundered in terror—
                they ran down the stairs
                    like chimneys of blood
                they caught the young men
                    in the dark cellars
                the places of slaughter
                    the animal sounds under the knife
                the kitchen midden
                    the black dank on the wall
all long ago—

there was a sharp instrument
                          a musical bow
I touched
                  it gave off a sound
disturbing the dust

they were hanged in the open air
                          wrapped in their grave cloths
a woman among them
her face crumpled
she swung as the mask moved
like the half of a nut it slipped from her face
                          it fell
the crowd breathed sharply
                          was still
horror   the mask fell
                  her face was the same

in her same face she will walk again
                  in the woods
                          in the house of her choice
I will meet her again in the shifting woods

Origin of the Peruvian Flute

A young man makes a flute out of his own
shin-bone to lament the death of his beloved.
Peruvian Legend

bitter leaves in my belly
under my tongue:
the knife is a sharp song
in my grief-mask I grin

blood sinks a dark root
my bone is clean as a moon
long and white I have carved it
a bird's throat to sing at her ear

I play for her dancing:
her breasts move like fruit on a bright tree
with my one foot I follow
to the forest, the river
with garlands I come

for her singing I play:
her voice is the slow water
the night-breath through leaves
to the dark god she journeys
my song is her path

The Messenger

Every five years the Thracians chose by lot a messenger to tell the gods of their needs. They sent him thus: three spears were held firm, the chosen man flung up into the air to fall on the spears. If he died the gods were favourable; if not, they sent another man.

in a spathe of silence
he moves
treading on worn stone,
what he was
herdsman, lover
he has forgotten,
self, like dross
sifted in the running stream

his skin no longer contains him
the subtle bones of his skull
move apart
out of his eyes he sees
only shadows
through white air
his spine
an avalanche of light

hands hover,
touch
what he no longer is

a huge flower opens
tremulous,
sky blooms;
parabola beyond eagles
lazy, infinite;

in his mind
periphery of dark,
the white curve
dispersing to zero

spears run like flame on water

on flung hills
an eagle descends

The Woman's Dream

A man and woman
alone in a vast sea,
companions of the water
swimming in grave delight.

They have forgotten the tree-fringed shore,
cannot imagine underfoot
pebbles or broken shell.
No looming rock, or fin or sail,
        or musky isle
disturb their calm.
The sea upholds them, shapes them;
their fragile plash scarce breaks its skin.

Their first sun rises,
spills at the sea's edge,
patterns the spread silk.
The man is all gold.
He gasps, he shimmers,
tosses up metallic drops,
his arms flash like swords.
He is robed and crowned in gold.
'To the sun', he calls, 'Come.'

The sun does not finger her;
the sea would whisper her in all oceans,
would speak through each orifice.
Currents probe at her thigh,
her blood is slower than tides,
a tongue of water has entered her throat.
She flails, falls back in shadow,
is succoured by sea-beasts—

dolphin, whale.
Summoned from unfathomable dark
they rise beneath her,
her belly flexed to the dolphin's curve.
She is borne, streaming,
into the miraculous, hurting air.

She does not turn to watch
where he, unmoving now,
is drowned, subsumed, in light.

Country Afternoon

we buy postcards
sepia-tinted
putting extra money, carefully, in the box

a lone tourist
made nervous by laughter
and the child climbing on tombstones
hurries towards the lych-gate
shuts it with an echoing click

a church noted by Betjeman
saddle-backed, herring-boned
tiny, cool
more ancient than its written history
a god's eye in Cotswold fields:
outside, the graven cross, six centuries worn
is a single shaft to heaven

from the crypt I look up
see your face for an instant
dark against sunlight
still as a stone knight

a wood-pigeon clatters—
from a smouldering bonfire
smoke wavers upwards
we gaze into the rectory orchard
heavy with forbidden fruit
dahlias in shocks lean towards us

across the lane
five geese from a fairy tale
cows gathered peaceably to be milked
a muddy ford with minnows
no sound or sight of other human

fifteen adults in this community
a few children and the old
where are they all—
indoors, or vanished long ago
into the hedgerows, the rolling fields?

at the edge of the wood a horse chases a cow

'an afternoon out of time,' you say
'fifty years or more ago
—if I built a church it would be like this'

I pick flowers that will not last the journey home

heat dances on tarmac
the child runs towards the car

where to go from here?

A Poet Visits
(for Yann)

Fields of foxy sorrel,
bedraggled nettle, ragwort,
yarrow juice on my hand.
'A good place to sit,'
                 you said.

Rain-mist drifts down hill,
hangs by the stream;
horses, muffled, shift and snort.
We reach out, floating, to touch the farthest tree.
'My wife and I move house.'

'A poet should name all names of bird and flower.'
You teach me "silena alba" for white campion.
—The summer trees turn bronze,
a scent of winter from the wood.
'No poem for three months,'
                 you said,
'the vision comes and goes.'

Walking in Autumn
(for Diana Lodge)

We have overshot the wood.
The track has led us beyond trees
to the tarmac edge. Too late now
at dusk to return a different way,
hazarding barbed wire or an unknown bull.
We turn back onto the darkening path.
Pale under-leaves of whitebeam, alder
gleam at our feet like stranded fish
or Hansel's stones.
A wren, unseen, churrs alarm:
each tree drains to blackness.
Halfway now, we know
by the leaning crab-apple;
feet crunching into mud
the hard slippery yellow moons.
We hurry without reason
stumbling over roots and stones.
A night creature lurches, cries out,
crashes through brambles.
Skin shrinks inside our clothes;
almost we run
falling through darkness to the wood's end,
the gate into the sloping field.
Home is lights and woodsmoke, voices—
and, our breath caught, not trembling now,
a strange reluctance to enter within doors.

Finding a Sheep's Skull

Sudden shock of bone
at the path's edge,
like a larger mushroom
almost hidden by leaves.

I handle the skull gently
shaking out earth and spiders.
Loose teeth chock in the jaw:
it smells of nothing.

I hold it up to sunlight,
a grey-green translucent shell.
Light pours in
    like water
through blades and wafers of bone.
    In secret caves
filaments of skull hang down;
frost and rain have worked
    to shredded lace.

The seasons waste its symmetry.
    It is a cathedral
echoing spring; in its decay
    plainsong of lamb
    and field and sun
inhabits bone.

The shallow cranium
fits in my palm

—for speculative children
I bring it home.

January

A sealed stillness
—only the stream moves,
tremor and furl of water
under dead leaves.

In silence
the wood declares itself:
angles and arabesques of darkness,
branch, bramble,
tussocks of ghost grass
—under my heel
ice shivers
frail blue as sky
between the runes of trees.

Far up
rooks, crows
flail home.

SNOW LIGHT, WATER LIGHT (1983)

for Roger and Adam
who shared the farmhouse

Poem found at Chesters Museum, Hadrian's Wall

To Jove, best and greatest
and to the other immortal gods;
to Augustus, happy and unconquered
Victory, holding a palm branch;
to Hadrian
commemorating 343 paces of the Roman Wall

> *bill hook, holdfast, trivet*
> *latch lifter, nail lifter, snaffle bit*
> *sickle blade, terret ring, spear butt*
> *boat hook, entrenching tool*
> *chisel, gouge, gimlet, punch*

To Longinus, trumpeter
and Milenus, standard bearer
1st Cohort of the Batavians;
to Cornelius Victor
served in the army 26 years
lived 55 years 11 days
erected by his wife;
to Brigomaglos, a Christian;
to my wife Aelia Comindus
who died aged 32

> *unguentaria*
> *balsamaria*
> *ivory comb*
> *pins of bronze and bone*
> *dress fastener*
> *strap fastener*
> *spinning whorls*
> *needles, spoons*
> *Millefiori beads*
> *ligula, earprobe*
> *tongs*

To the woodland god Cocidius;
to Coventina, water goddess
and attendant nymphs

  —*in her well*
  axe hammer
  spiral ring, jet ring
  dogbrooch, coins

To the Mother Goddesses
to the gods of this place
to the goddesses across the water
to the old gods
to a god . . .

dedication partly obliterated
with human figure in rude relief
text of doubtful meaning
dedication illegible

uninscribed

stone of . . .

Brigomaglos, a Christian, Speaks . . .

'Some say they saw the Bull,
stamping under the skyline
with the new sun rising between his horns.
They say the black blood flows like water . . .

I don't believe them.
It was only the officers,
        never the men
(any god would do for us
        till the White Christ came).
They'd see anything, anyway,
stumbling out of their caves
dizzy with darkness and the stink of blood.

Strange how they thought they brought the light to birth.

We pulled their temple down in the end,
opened it up to the proper light
—plenty of black birds flapping around
but never their Raven that flies to the sun.

We have the Sun,
our Christ is the Son who is brought to birth.
He is a white Dove
        who walks in fields of light,
brighter than snow-light or water-light.
His light burns in us.
He has engraved our souls like glass
to hold his seeds of light.

Those old gods should keep their place
under the dark of stones
or in the deep wood.
They should fade like the last wood-ember
or the last sputtering flame of the lamp,
be echoed only in children's songs.

In sleep they crowd
riding the uneasy edge of dreams . . .'

*The Mithraic Temple at Carrawburgh is believed
to have been pulled down by Christians in A.D.297.*

Vindolanda – January

     winter light
a track through trees
leaning with frozen snow;
boy and dogs whoop ahead,
in a white flurry
vanish over the near horizon

     slush, mud underfoot
the sign-post obscured

     Vindolanda
a word warm on the tongue
—voices returning
bronze glint by firelight
smoke from the hill

     over the black burn
through stark trees
a stone tower
     white shrouded,
blue shadowed humps in the land

     birds hop, silent
a moon sharpens the yellow sky

     snow drives into the angled field

     on the map of the land
boy, dogs wheel and turn
perspectives away

Stone

      iron-culled
obdurate harvest

      endures our purpose
without blood or cry

      sundered, hewn
can stone give comfort to stone?

      outlasts flame, petal, bone

is the sleep of stars

      will ripen to its own season

Irthing Valley

a field of stones
a river of stones

each stone in its place

can a star be lost
or a stone?

uncountable
the constellations of stone

the wind lays itself down
                                        at dusk
a fine cloth over the stones

the river is dispossessed
it casts up white branches
                                        roots
shoals of white sand

it cannot oust its stones

between air and water
                                        my shadow
laving the stones

The Crooked Glen

I saw nothing but waves and winds

> . . . the moon resting in a broken apple tree
> an ushering wind shake ash and alder
> by the puckered river.
> Lightly, like boats, the thin leaves rock and spin.

Blood-dark berries stir; above my head the thorn trees lean.
In their black pools the moon fragments herself.

Ghost dry the unquiet reeds . . .

I saw nothing but the waters wap
and waves wan

Camboglanna or the Crooked Glen is one
of the reputed sites of Arthur's last battle.

Flowers
(for Winifred Nicholson)

    Flowers,
a dozen or more,
I picked one summer afternoon
from field and hedgerow.
Resting against a wall
I held them up
to hide the sun.
Cell by cell,
exact as dance,
I saw the colour,
structure, purpose
of each flower.
I named them with their secret names.
They flamed in air.

    But, waking
I remember only two
—soapwort and figwort,
the lilac and the brown.
The rest I guess at
but cannot see
—only myself,
almost a ghost upon the road,
without accoutrement,
holding the flowers
as torch and talisman
against the coming dark.

For Stephen Procter
on seeing his exhibition of forms in glass

Perfected whiteness
—a stellar littoral, bright
beyond bone or pearl.

Spiral chambers sing of
sea's breath, the curve
and fall of flowers.

Cave within a cave
of quiet, thought becomes music;
litanies of light resolve

in gathering trance.
A whorl of shadow
trembles, brims.

Oh wave and silence,
breaking still
in shining arcs of air.

Sightings

Flake on flake, snow
packed light as ash
              or feather,
shavings of crystal.
      By moonlight
stars pulse underfoot.

The burning fox ran here,
his narrow print
      under gate
              and over wall
diagonal across the field;
      skeining of rabbit tracks,
our own slurred trail.

Like black stones
crows squat, sunning
      among staring sheep
—crow's wing
      brushed on snow,
three strokes
      twice etched
as faint and fine
      as fossil bone.

Rain – Birdoswald

I stand under a leafless tree
more still, in this mouse-pattering
    thrum of rain,
than cattle shifting in the field.
    It is more dark than light.
A Chinese painter's brush of deepening grey
    moves in a subtle tide.

    The beasts are darker islands now.
Wet-stained and silvered by the rain
    they suffer night,
marooned as still as stone or tree.
    We sense each other's quiet.

    Almost, death could come
inevitable, unstrange
    as is this dusk and rain,
and I should be no more
    myself, than raindrops
glimmering in last light
    on black ash buds

or night beasts in a winter field.

VOICES RETURNING

for Roger and Adam

Chrysalis

Not bud, not seed;
   a small horn
pointed, grooved
   all winter
you clung above the stove
   heraldic.
Sometimes I laid my finger on you
   and felt a spasm
   deep-rooted
as though from my own flesh.
We did not know your hidden state
   dull moth or emperor.

   Indoors
a steady warmth.
   You became yourself.
The first day of spring
   we saw the empty tomb
the husk
   still fastened to the wall
you, risen
   interleaved with air
plain cabbage white
   but green veined, delicate.

We open windows.
Outside, leaves whipped on stone
    shut celandines
—no scented harbourage
on plant or wall.
    You choose this room
your house of airy change
    practise your set dance
await the sun.

    But in the morning
wings shredded to a blur
we find you on the kitchen floor.
    The cats are nonchalant.
What omen this, the second day?
What shaken web that meshes us
    humans, cats, butterfly
in a cold spring?

For Adam, nearly twelve

Each spring
reminds of other springs.
This, your last April
as a child,
I remember visiting friends
in your first month.
You, bleating in the house,
lamb cry from the fields,
I rushed indoors and out
not knowing which
my full breasts spurting milk.
I am photographed
through hawthorn flowers
unfocussed, blurred
by blossom,
my face not yet my own.

Driving home
a lorry tailed too closely
down a hill.
From my rear mirror
it seemed huge cab
and tyres one inch away
from you, asleep.
I drew in.
Trembling at the wheel
I wept and swore
at all machines and men
that threatened you

as I still do.

Romeo and Juliet at the Old Vic

A clear flame
now still
now trembling
on the empty stage

Desire remote to us
thirteen year olds
from shabby Walthamstow
tittering in the balcony.
I, fierce, hissing in the dark
'Shut up, you fools'
yearned through shafts of light
to that white face
that fluting bird's voice
passion snared

Tearless, rapt
with secret flowering grief
I stumbled down stone steps
vowed to beauty & to love

Death? We knew
the mimic lovers rose again.
The long and little deaths of love
we could not know,
not Juliet, nor us
nor that young actress
famous now,
ageing, twice divorced
burning still
beyond her brilliant masks

Letter to My Son

Twelve years ago
still you danced your cosmic dance
within the waters of my womb.
At night you kicked and pummelled
with heel and fist.
Both of us travelled towards the unknown.
Then I remember in a white and sterile room
you ripping me apart
and held up by heels
your first cry a chime of silver bells
your genitals like some rare orchid.

Now I lie again in a white and sterile room
my body racked and torn
but not by birth.
I cry to God
to give you strength,
to comfort you
and others that I love.
But if you were sitting by this bed,
which I do not wish,
I could say to you,
Adam, do you remember this?
and you would say,
Yes, Mummy,
or Frances, as you call me now,
and then, do you remember how we did this
and I said that
and then we both went here
and I saw this?

I wonder who would remember most?
I, I think
—and this, your early body, soul and mind,
hold me to myself
when all else falls apart.
The memories are mine:
the rest of you I let go free,
my child who will be a man.

Evening

          Lilac blossom crests the window sill
mingling whiteness with the good dark of this room.
A bloom of light hangs delicately in white painted angles.
Bluebells heaped in a pot
still hold their blue against the dark;
I see their green stalks glisten.

          Thin as a swan's bone
I wait for the lessons of pain and light.
Grief is a burden, useless.
It must dissolve into the dark.
I see the hills, luminous.
There will be the holly tree
the hawthorn with mistletoe
foxgloves springing in thousands.

The hills also will pass away
          will remain
as this lilac light, these blue bells,
the good dark of this room.

UNFINISHED POEMS
AND FRAGMENTS

Irthing River

pewter
   delicately beaten
      a child's eye tremor
of milky blue

glimmer of oils
over roots and sodden grass
   silk skin
      slides opaque
sloughs into rills

a caressing of tongues
      over stone
such laving—
wind become visible
     clothing the stone

vortices, like flowers
   suck air
      suck light

*A draft of a poem Frances was working on shortly before
she wrote 'Irthing Valley' in* Snow Light, Water Light. *
One or two of the images are echoed in 'Irthing Valley'.*

Sketch

    Yielded to windless air
a frail November harebell
     rests in a glass
Its stem leans stiffly
    Sucking the quiet water
in less-than-outdoor cold
    one bud unscrolls its fluted blue

Another draft from the time of Snow Light, Water Light:
*written at Kiln Hill, the farmhouse on Hadrian's Wall,
towards the end of 1981.*

Orkney

a scapular of sea
between islands: smooth, shining
   as thin bone

feather, mouse-skull, broken
       chambered shell
the clean death
   by water and salt wind

a roofless cottage
   from the dark door space flying
lapwing or whitemaa

your eyes, my eyes
   the colour of these islands
a travelling grey

*From a notebook Frances kept on a visit to Orkney
in April 1982. As so often, she made her notes in
the form of haiku or near-haiku.*

Wilson Ward

earless
eyeless
noseless
we drift on
in our lonely beds
the old one
Mrs Rivers
eighty five
floats out
sans everything

*Written in hospital in August 1983: 'that's all
I can manage at the moment.'*

Orcop Haiku

Garway Hill through rain
    —my September window pane
glass beads flung on glass

*The last poem that Frances wrote. For some months
she had been confined to bed, her world restricted
to the view through the window.*

Bibliographical note

The High Tower (New Departures, 1970) contained sixteen poems, four of them—'Loving You', 'Bird', 'Omen' and 'Morning Waking'—reprinted from Frances' first pamphlet *Poems* (St Albert's Press, 1967) which contained twelve poems. I have omitted 'Omen' but added two other poems from *Poems*, 'Do you not know . . .' and 'Love Poem', and one uncollected poem, 'Buzzard', which was written in 1969.

Water Over Stone (Enitharmon Press, 1980) contained thirty-three poems, four of them—'Dream', 'Moon', 'Spell' and 'Crow'—reprinted from *The High Tower*. I have omitted one poem, 'Cerne Abbas', from the series commissioned by Gallery 5, but added four other poems from the same series— 'Chanctonbury Ring', 'West Kennet Long Barrow', 'Uffington White Horse', and 'Glastonbury Tor'—and a further fourteen uncollected poems: 'Spring', 'Invocation', 'Solstice Song', "blaze blaze summer moon"', 'August Full Moon', 'Storm', 'Night-piece', "last light withdraws"', 'Elegy for the Mummy of a Young Girl in the British Museum', 'Old Song', 'Written in the Black Mountains', 'Poem in Spring', 'Country Afternoon', and 'A Poet Visits'. I have also included 'Finding a Sheep's Skull' and 'January' which were published in *Snow Light, Water Light* (Bloodaxe Books, 1983) but written towards the end of Frances' ten years in Gloucestershire.

With the exception of those two poems, *Snow Light, Water Light* is reprinted complete.

The five poems in 'Voices Returning' were all written in the course of 1983, 'Letter to My Son' in the Royal Marsden Hospital, the others in Herefordshire.

R.G.

Index of Titles and First Lines

Frances Horovitz was born in 1938 in London. Her maiden name was Frances Hooker. She read English and Drama at Bristol University and trained as an actress at the Royal Academy of Dramatic Art. After some work in television and repertory, she concentrated on developing the art of poetry reading and became widely known for her readings on radio and in live performance. In 1975 she was one of a cast of four chosen to give the first performance of Ted Hughes's *Cave Birds* at the Ilkley Festival. In a long and successful partnership with Robert Gittings, the biographer of Keats and Hardy, she presented Keats and Hardy in platform performances at the National Theatre and at numerous arts festivals. Among many fine recordings for BBC Radio 3, her readings of Russian women poets in three programmes called *Among the Witnesses* were particularly notable. She also made a number of recordings for the Open University.

The impetus to write herself came after her marriage to the poet Michael Horovitz in 1964. Her first pamphlet, *Poems*, was published in 1967 and her second, *The High Tower*, in 1970. In 1971 her son Adam was born and the family moved to Gloucestershire, to a remote thumb off-shoot of the Slad Valley, the source of many of the poems in her first full-length collection, *Water Over Stone* (1980). She became greatly valued as a poetry tutor, working particularly for the Arvon Foundation. BBC 2 made a television film of her work as a Poet in Schools which was shown in 1981.

In December 1980 she moved to the North of England, where she joined the poet Roger Garfitt in working on *Wall* (LYC Press, 1981), an exploration by four poets and four artists of the theme of Hadrian's Wall. For two winters they rented a farmhouse at Kiln Hill, near the Roman fort of Birdoswald. They became closely associated with the nearby LYC Gallery, where she met Winifred Nicholson, and several of the artists with whom she contributed to a new landscape anthology, *Presences of Nature* (Carlisle Museum & Art Gallery, 1982). The Irthing Valley below Birdoswald was the source of most of the poems in her third pamphlet, *Snow Light, Water Light* (1983).

In July 1982 they moved to Herefordshire, a landscape she had known and written about since the late sixties, and which had already become the setting for *Rowlstone Haiku* (Five Seasons Press, 1982). Her life there was immediately overshadowed by the onset of cancer of the ear. She married Roger Garfitt shortly before her death in October 1983.

Her death was marked by a series of memorial readings, and by the publication of two commemorative pamphlets, *Tenfold* (Martin Booth, 1983) and *A Celebration of and for Frances Horovitz* (New Departures, 2nd Edition, 1984).

Winifred Nicholson was born in 1893. She was the granddaughter of the 9th Earl of Carlisle, a painter and friend of the Pre-Raphaelites. After attending the Byam Shaw and Camden Hill art schools—and also studying in Paris—she travelled to India, and there developed her love of colour.

In 1920 she married the painter Ben Nicholson and lived with him in Cumbria and Paris, wintering in Castagnola, where they often painted side by side in the snow. The Nicholsons exhibited at the Paterson Gallery, London, in 1927, and were members of the 7 & 5 Society from 1928 to 1935. Following a visit by Christopher Wood to Cumbria, they gathered in Cornwall and painted there with other artists of the new St Ives group.

In Paris during the 1930s Winifred Nicholson met Mondrian, Brancussi, Arp and others, and was experimenting with abstraction. She returned to Cumbria at the outbreak of war. After the war she developed her landscape work, making use of abstract discoveries in her flower paintings and in landscapes with rainbows. She died in 1981.

The cover painting is 'Night Window—Isle of Wight' (*circa* 1931), oil on canvas, 24" × 24", reproduced by kind permission of Kate Nicholson.